First published 2009 by order of the Tate Trustees
by Tate Publishing, a division of Tate Enterprises Ltd,
Millbank, London SW1P 4RG
www.tate.org.uk/publishing

A catalogue record for this book is available from the British Library

ISBN 978 1 85437 816 3 (hbk)

Distributed in the United States and Canada by
Harry N. Abrams, Inc., New York

Library of Congress Control Number: 2009931142

Photography by Marcus Leith and Andrew Dunkley

Designed by Peter Blake and Coriander Studio with
Geoffrey Winston at Graphics with Art

Colour reproduction by DL Interactive, London

Printed in China by C&C

Mixed Sources
Product group from well-managed
forests, controlled sources and
recycled wood or fiber
www.fsc.org Cert no. SGS-COC-003548
© 1996 Forest Stewardship Council
FSC

Endpapers: Detail from Peter Blake, *The Toy Shop* 1962, Tate

Photograph of Peter Blake © Philip Sinden

PETER BLAKE'S
ABC

Tate Publishing

IS FOR APPLE

IS FOR BICYCLE

IS FOR CAT

IS FOR DOG

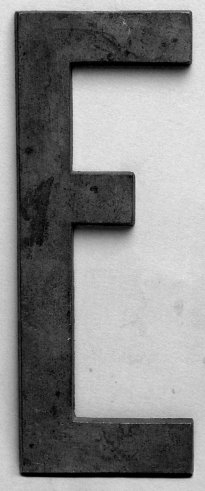

IS FOR ELEPHANT

IS FOR FAN

IS FOR GNOME

IS FOR HORSE

IS FOR ICE

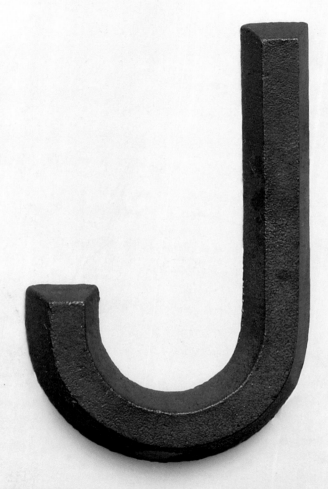

IS FOR JUG

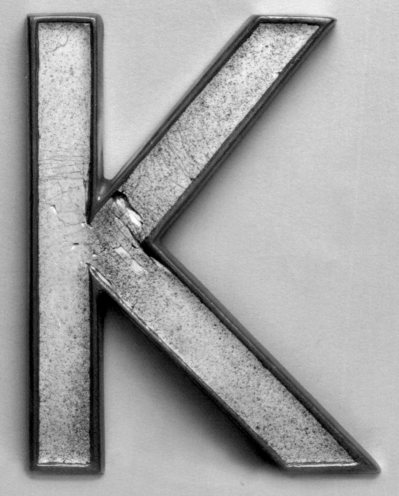

IS FOR KNOTS

Cadenilla

Margarita

Margarita

Llano

Vuelta de bita

Vuelta mordida

IS FOR LOCOMOTIVE

IS FOR MOTOR CAR

IS FOR NUMBERS

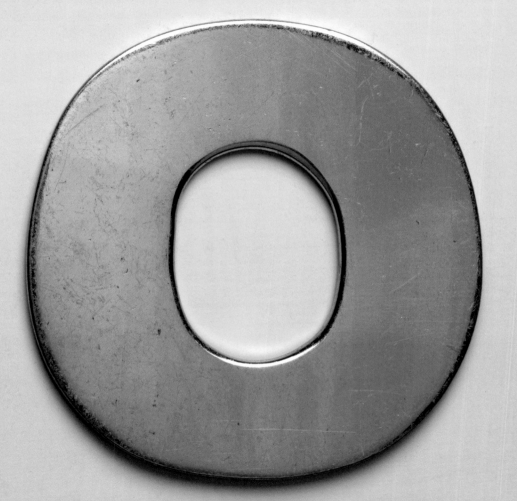

IS FOR ORCHESTRA

IS FOR PUNCH

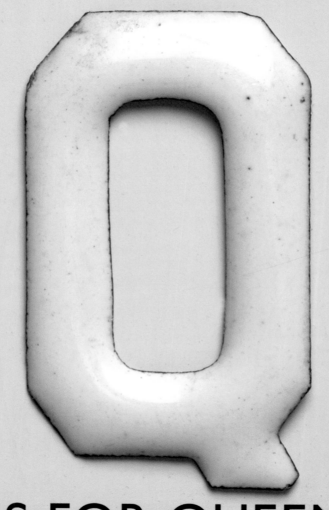

IS FOR QUEEN

ELIZABETH II
1953

IS FOR RATTLE

IS FOR SHOES

IS FOR TRUCK

IS FOR UNION JACK

IS FOR VIKING

IS FOR WHISTLE

IS FOR XMAS

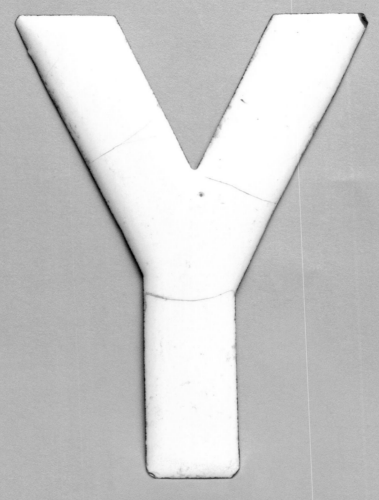

IS FOR YACHT

IS FOR ZEBRA

A note from the artist

When I was asked to make an ABC book, my immediate reaction was that all the pictures could come from my collection of toys and objects. What I found interesting was that an elderly adult would be choosing things for the eyes of children, but also for grown-ups who could enjoy them in a nostalgic way. Some of these objects are unusual, as I didn't want to 'talk down' to my younger readers. I hope you enjoy them as much as I do.

Peter Blake.